Halloween Recipes

Delicious Recipes for a Special Occasion

(Your Spooky Cookbook of Creepy but Tasty Dish Ideas)

Patricia Smith

Published By **Simon Dough**

Patricia Smith

All Rights Reserved

Halloween Recipes: Delicious Recipes for a Special Occasion (Your Spooky Cookbook of Creepy but Tasty Dish Ideas)

ISBN 978-1-77485-953-7

No part of this guidebook shall be reproduced in any form without permission in writing from the publisher except in the case of brief quotations embodied in critical articles or reviews.

Legal & Disclaimer

The information contained in this ebook is not designed to replace or take the place of any form of medicine or professional medical advice. The information in this ebook has been provided for educational & entertainment purposes only.

The information contained in this book has been compiled from sources deemed reliable, and it is accurate to the best of the Author's knowledge; however, the Author cannot guarantee its accuracy and validity and cannot be held liable for any errors or omissions. Changes are periodically made to this book. You must consult your doctor or get professional medical advice before using any of the suggested remedies, techniques, or information in this book.

Upon using the information contained in this book, you agree to hold harmless the Author from and against any damages, costs, and expenses, including any legal fees potentially resulting from the application of any of the information provided by this guide. This disclaimer applies to any damages or injury caused by the use and application, whether directly or indirectly, of any advice or information presented, whether for breach of contract, tort, negligence, personal injury, criminal intent, or under any other cause of action.

You agree to accept all risks of using the information presented inside this book. You need to consult a professional medical practitioner in order to ensure you are both able and healthy enough to participate in this program.

Table of contents

Grapefruit Jack-O'-Lanterns 1

Chocolate Apple Halloween Owl 3

Monster S'mores 6

Silly Apple Bites 8

Witch Hat Peanut Butter Cookies 10

Mini Chocolate Bat Bites 13

Hats & Bats Chocolate-Peanut Butter Tarts 15

Marshmallow Ghost Brownies 19

Coffin Sandwich Cookies 24

Nutter Butter Boos 28

Towering Haunted House Cake 30

Something-To-Hide Devil's Food Cupcakes 35

Licorice-Eared Mice Mini-Cakes 40

Spiced Chocolate Bat Cookies 43

Peanut Butter Acorns 47

Spooky Fingers 50

Banana Mummies 52

Pumpkin Rice Krispies Treats 56

Candy Corn Chocolate Chip Cookie Cake 60

Spooky Halloween Pretzels 64

Haunted Haystacks 67

Candy Corn White Chocolate M&M Blondies .. 70

Halloween Pumpkin Cookie Cake 73

Halloween Sprinkle Cookies 75

Halloween Chocolate Chip Cookies 79

Pumpkin Pretzels With Jack-O-Lantern Faces For Halloween 83

Chocolate Monster Halloween Cookies 86

Spider Oreo Balls 91

Boo-Nilla Ghost Milkshakes 94

Halloween Deviled Eggs 96

Witch's Kid-Friendly Halloween Brew 99

Scary Butternut Squash Spider Web Soup 101

Classic Dirt Cake 104

Melted Mud Chocolate 106

Spooky Spider Cookies 108

- Evil Spirit Pops 110
- Witch Hat Cookies 111
- Pumpkin Cheesecake Dip 114
- Classic Dirt Cake 116
- Pumpkin Face Quesadillas 118
- Pumpkin Face Quesadillas 120
- Halloween Pumpkin Spice Bars 122
- Mummy Hot Dogs 125
- Witch Hat Cookies 127
- Crispy Devil Brains 128
- Melted Witch 130
- Killing Apple Punch 131
- Halloween Pumpkin Spice Bars 132
- Mummy Hot Dogs 134
- Poison Apple Candy 136
- Spiced Roasted Pumpkin Seeds 138
- Oreo Dirt Cups 140
- Glass Jelly Worms 142

Frozen Banana Ghosts 144

Spider Sandwich Cookies 145

Mysterious Strawberries 147

Dead Eyeballs 149

Zombie Cocktail 150

Good And Wicked Brew 152

Blood Margarita 154

Scary Zombie Fingers 156

Festering Apples 158

Caramel Nut Tart 160

Guacamoldy Eyeballs 166

Ghost Toast 169

Halloween Creepy Skull Cupcakes 171

Witch Hat Cookies 174

Grave Yard Taco Dip 176

Pumpkin Cinnamon Halloween Cookies 179

Snakes Bites ...... **Error! Bookmark not defined.**

Cheese Pumpkins**Error! Bookmark not defined.**

Grapefruit Jack-O'-Lanterns

Recipes
1. 3 large apples
2. 2 medium oranges
3. 2 large lemons, juiced
4. 1 cup of grapefruit chunks
5. 1 teaspoon cinnamon
6. 1 tablespoon maple syrup
7. 1 tablespoon honey
8. ½ – ¾ cup pistachios
9. 1 tablespoon craisins
10. 2 tablespoon golden raisins

Procedures

1. Using a serrated knife to cut out a top and then scoop the insides out. Save the top and as big of chunks as you can for the salad, and anything leftover you can use to make my favourite <u>grapefruit sorbet</u>
2. With a small pairing knife, Try carving out a jack-o-lantern face.
3. Fill it with Fall Harvest Salad (recipes above).

Chocolate Apple Halloween Owl

Yields: 8 servings and Total time: 12 minutes

Recipes

1. 2 apples

2. 1 bag semisweet chocolate chips 23 oz

3. 8 wooden sticks 6-inch

4. 1 bag standard-sized Oreos

5. 8 Candy Corns for the nose

6. Wilton Candy Eyeballs

7. Ribbons

Procedures

1. Put apples upright on a wood board and slice from top to bottom (about 4 slices per apple, half-inch thick). Remove seeds with caution. At that point, line a large cookie sheet with aluminum foil & push each stick's pointed end up into the bottom of each apple slice.
2. In a medium bowl (should be glass), melt chocolate chips in the microwave according to the package directions, Put the bowl into a larger bowl which is filled with about two-inch boiling water (this will prevent the chocolate from hardening), and dip apple slices in chocolate using a spoon to help cover each slice if your bowl isn't deep enough to cover them.
3. You should allow excess chocolate to drip off, then lay flat on the foil-lined baking sheet. Use the Oreos to decorate both the ears and eyes of the

owl & the candy corn for the nose while chocolate is still wet. Use a small dot of melted chocolate as glue for the candy eyeballs.

4. Place the baking sheet in the refrigerator for about ten-fifteen minutes, allowing chocolate to harden. However, If you wish, decorate the wood stick with a ribbon. Serve chocolate-apple Halloween owl and enjoy it!

Monster S'mores

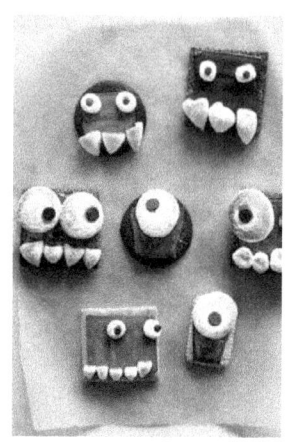

Recipes & Supplies
1.Parchment paper assorted flat cookies (such as honey or chocolate graham crackers, Nabisco Famous Chocolate Wafers, and tea biscuits)
2.Thin flat chocolate bars (such as Hershey's)
3.Scissors
4.Regular and mini marshmallows

5. toothpick
6. regular and mini chocolate chips

Procedures

1. Preheat the broiler. 2. Line a baking sheet with parchment papeer. Place the cookies on the baking sheet & put a piece of the chocolate bar on top of each one. 3. To make the eyes, cut mini or regular marshmallows in half horizontally. Arrange the halves on top of the chocolate, sticky side down. Poke holes in the marshmallows with the toothpick, and dig around to enlarge the holes. Push a mini or regular chocolate chip into each hole, pointy side down. 4. To make the teeth, cut angled pieces of the remaining mini or regular marshmallows and press the cut sides into the chocolate. You should put the baking sheet in the oven and observe. Remove as soon as the s'mores turn golden, about 45 seconds. They turn golden very quickly, in as fast as 45 seconds, and can burn before you know it,

so stay right next to the oven with your oven mitt on! Let them cool until they're just warm before handling or eating. Enjoy!

Silly Apple Bites

Recipes
1. 2 green apples, each quartered
2. sunflower butter
3. 32 sunflower seeds
4. 2–3 strawberries, sliced
5. 1–2 homemade googly eyes per apple bite

Procedures
1. Carve the middles out of each quarter of the apple to create a mouth. However, you don't have to worry about perfection, you will fill the gaps with sunbutter anyway so if you accidentally carve too deep, It can be easily covered up.

2. The cut gap inside should be coated with a filling of sunflower butter.
3. Place four sunflower seeds on the top of the "mouth" for the teeth.
4. Place one sliced strawberry inside the mouth for the tongue.
5. Each eye above the mouth should be glued with a dab of sun butter to stick.
6. Serve with a smile. Enjoy!

Witch Hat Peanut Butter Cookies

Recipes

1. 48 Hershey's Kisses Brand Milk Chocolates
2. 1/2 Cup Shortening
3. 1 Cup Creamy Peanut Butter
4. 1/2 Cup Packed Light Brown Sugar
5. 1/3 Cup Granulated Sugar
6. 1 Egg
7. 2 Tablespoons Milk

8. 1 Teaspoon Vanilla Extract
9. 1 Cup All-Purpose Flour
10. 1/3 Cup Hershey's Cocoa
11. 1 Teaspoon Baking Soda
12. 1/2 Teaspoon Salt
13. 1/3 Cup Black Sugar Sprinkles For Rolling
14. 1/2 Cup Chocolate Chips
15. Decorative Sprinkles

Procedures

1. Heat oven to 375°F. Remove wrappers from chocolates.
2. Beat shortening & peanut butter in a large bowl until well blended. Add brown sugar and 1/3 cup granulated sugar; beat until fluffy. Add Egg, milk, and vanilla; beat well. Stir together flour, cocoa, baking soda, and salt; gradually beat into peanut butter mixture.

3. Shape dough into 1-inch balls. Roll in black sugar sprinkles; place on ungreased cookie sheet.

4. Bake eight to ten minutes or until set. Immediately press a chocolate into the center of each cookie; the cookie will crack around the edges. Remove from cookie sheet to wire rack. Cool completely.

5. Melt chocolate chips in 30-second intervals until melted. Let cool slightly. Carefully pour into a ziploc bag and cut off the tip. Pipe melted chocolate around kisses and immediately sprinkle Halloween sprinkles on it. It should make about 48 cookies. Enjoy!

Mini Chocolate Bat Bites

Yield: 25 servings or more and Total time: 15 minutes

Recipes

1. 25 Miniature Reeses Cups
2. 25 Thin Oreo Chocolate Sandwich Cookies
3. 1/3 cup storebought cream cheese frosting (or homemade, if you can)
4. 50 Edible/Eatable eyes

Procedures

1. Take out the wrappers from the Reeses cups.
2. Shatter the cookies in half & then separate all of the pieces from one another, so you now have 4 "bat wings." Scrape off the frosting & discard (or eat!)
3. Fill a plastic bag with the store-bought or homemade frosting. Cut off the tip of the bag & pipe frosting onto the back corners of the broken cookie pieces.
4. Press 1 cookie piece on the right and left of the Reeses cup.
5. Pipe frosting on the back of the edible eyes & secure on top of the center of the Reeses cup. Enjoy!

Hats & Bats Chocolate-Peanut Butter Tarts

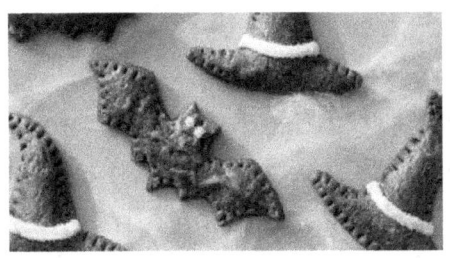

Yield: 20 servings and Total time: 3 hours 5 minutes

Recipe
1. Half cup of smooth peanut butter
2. Half cup of confectioners' sugar
3. 1/3 cup of mini chocolate chips.
4. Two cups of all-purpose flour, spooned and leveled, and more for the work surface.
5. ¼ cup of unsweetened cocoa powder.
6. 3 tablespoons of granulated sugar.
7. ½ teaspoon of kosher salt.
8. ½ cup of cold unsalted butter chopped into smaller pieces.

9. 8 ounces (1 package) of cold cream cheese, cut into smaller pieces, and store-bought white frosting and white sanding sugar for decorating.

Procedures

1. Gently stir together the confectioners' sugar and peanut butter in a clean bowl until it becomes smooth and gives a dough form. And stir in chocolate chips.
2. Pulse together cocoa powder, the granulated sugar, flour, and salt in a food processor up to four times.
3. Add the pulse and butter until the butter becomes the size of peas up to six times.
4. Add cream cheese and pulse until it forms dough up to twelve times. (add one to two tablespoons of water if needed to help the dough form well).
5. Divide dough into 2 pieces and wrap it in plastic wrap.
6. In a flattened shape, chill at least for one hour and leave for up to two days.

7. Gently preheat the oven to 350°f. Then line two baking sheets with clean parchment paper. Gently roll out dough to 1/8-inch thick on a lightly clean floured work surface.
8. Cut out shapes with 3-inch witch hat & bat cookie cutters.
9. Gently place half of each shape, 1/2-inch apart, on an organized baking sheet. Top it with peanut butter filling, leaving a small border around the edge. Then brush edges with clean water & place a duplicate cut-out on the top. Crimp the edges with a fork.
10. Bake it until cooked through, up to ten minutes.
11. Transfer it to a wire rack and allow to cool completely.
12. Gently place a small amount of white frosting in a clean zip-top bag, snip a small hole in one corner—pipe eyes on bats & a band on the witch hats.

Then sprinkle with sanding sugar.

Marshmallow Ghost Brownies

Yields: 12- 16 servings ETA: 2 hours and 50 mins

Recipe

For Brownies:

1. One cup and two tablespoons of all-purpose flour, leveled and spooned.
2. Cooking spray.
3. One and a half teaspoon of pumpkin pie spice.
4. ½ teaspoon of kosher salt.
5. ¼ teaspoon of baking powder
6. ¼ cup of unsweetened cocoa powder.
7. One cup semisweet chocolate chip.
8. One and a half cup of sugar
9. Nine tablespoons of unsalted butter.

One teaspoon of pure vanilla extract.

Three large eggs

¾ cup of pumpkin puree

For the Marshmallow Ghosts:
1. Half cup of granulated sugar.
2. 1 ¼ teaspoon of unflavored gelatin.
3. Store-bought black piping frosting.

Procedures:

Preparing the Brownies:
1. Gently preheat the oven to 350°F. Also, line a 9- by 13-inch pan with clean parchment paper, leaving a 2-inch overhang on the two long sides. Gently grease paper.
2. Gently whisk the pie spice, flour, salt, and baking powder in a bowl altogether.
3. Gently Melt chocolate chips, cocoa, and butter in a small clean saucepan over medium heat, then occasionally stirring, until smooth, up to three minutes.
4. Whisk the eggs, pumpkin puree, salt, and vanilla in a separate clean bowl

altogether. Add butter mixture to sugar mixture & stir gently to combine.
5. Gently add flour mixture & stir to combine. Transfer to the prepared clean, dry pan.
6. Keep baking until a clean toothpick inserted in the middle comes out with a few moist crumbs attached; cook for up to thirty minutes. Move to a wire rack & cool off completely in pan. Gently run a knife along the two short sides of the pan & lift brownies from the pan using clean parchment. Remove parchment & transfer brownies to a serving platter.

How to make Marshmallow Ghosts:
1. Gently sprinkle gelatin over 1/4 cup of cold water in a clean bowl to soften.
2. Then combine sugar & 1/4 cup of water in a small clean saucepan. Cook over medium-high heat, keep stirring until sugar is dissolved, up to two minutes.

3. Once the water comes to a boil, halt stirring, & wash downsides of the pan with a clean wet pastry brush to remove any undissolved sugar & prevent crystals from forming.
4. Proceed to boil until the temperature reaches 238°F on a candy thermometer, up to six minutes.
5. Add the sugar mixture to the gelatin. Gently whisk with an electric mixer on medium speed for three minutes. Increase speed to high & whisk till soft peaks form, up to ten minutes.
6. Then transfer the marshmallow to a clean heavy-duty zip-top bag with a tiny hole cut in one corner.
7. Instantly pipe ghost shapes on the brownies. Allow it to dry for one hour.
8. Then Pipe black frosting eyes & mouths.
9. Brownies can be stored in a clean airtight container for one day.

The marshmallows are best completed in a clean small saucepan. If the sugar combination does not reach the bulb on your candy thermometer, simply adjust the pan to bring it up to the level.

Coffin Sandwich Cookies

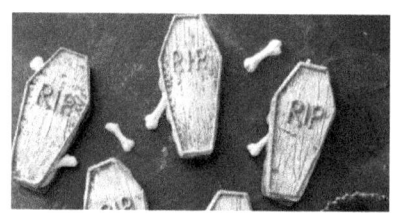

Yields: 34 servings and ETA is three hours, forty-five minutes

Recipes:

To make the Cookies:
1. Two tablespoons of unsweetened cocoa powder.
2. ¾ teaspoon kosher salt.
3. 1/3 cups of cornstarch.
4. ½ cup of molasses.
5. One cup of packed light brown sugar.
6. One cup of softened unsalted butter.
7. Five cups of all-purpose flour, leveled and spooned.
8. Two large eggs.

To make the White Chocolate Bones:
1. ½ cup of white chocolate candy melts.

To make the Buttercream Filling:
1. ¼ teaspoon of pure vanilla extract.
2. 1 ½ cups of sifted confectioners' sugar.
3. ½ cup of softened unsalted butter.
4. Orange food coloring.
5. A pinch of kosher salt.
6. Red food coloring.

To make the Royal Icing.
1. Two cups of confectioners' sugar.
2. Black food coloring.
3. Two tablespoons of Meringue powder.

Procedures
1. In making the cookies, gently preheat the oven to 375°f.
2. Line four baking sheets with clean parchment paper.
3. Whisk together cocoa, cornstarch, & salt in a bowl.
4. Gently beat butter & sugar with an electric mixer on medium speed until it becomes light & fluffy, up to four minutes.

5. Then kindly add molasses & beat until incorporated, up to one minute.
6. Ensure you beat in eggs, one at a time, scraping the bottom & sides of the bowl after each addition. Reduce mixer speed to medium-low & beat in cornstarch mixture. Beat in flour just up until it's incorporated. Then divide the dough into 2 pieces & wrap in plastic wrap; flatten. Chill at least one hour and up to 2 days.
7. Gently roll dough to 3/8-inch thickness on a clean floured work surface. Then cut coffin shapes with a 3-inch coffin cookie cutter, then move to prepare the baking sheets. Keep baking until cookies are set around all the edges but still a little soft in the center, up to eight minutes.
8. Kindly make white chocolate bones and melt candy melts following the package instructions. Move to a zip-top bag & snip a tiny hole in one corner. Fill up

the bone mold with melted candies. Then chill until firm; this should take up to thirty minutes. Gently tap out of the molds.
9. Make the filling by beating butter with an electric mixer on medium speed till it becomes smooth & creamy; this will take up to two minutes. Then add confectioners' sugar, a half cup at a time, mixing well & scraping down sides of bowl frequently. Beat in salt and vanilla. Make use of red & orange food coloring to dye into deep orange color.

To make the royal icing, gently combine confectioners' sugar & meringue powder in a clean bowl. Then add one and a half tablespoons of water & stir to mix.

Nutter Butter Boos

Yields: 12 servings Total time: 20 minutes
Recipes
1. Twelve nutter Butter Cookies
2. 2 cups Almond Bark or White chocolate, finely chopped
3. 1/2 cup chocolate, finely chopped

Procedures
1. Place the almond bark or white chocolate in a microwavable bowl or mug.

2. Put or Lay your cookies out on a piece of wax or parchment paper, or prop them up using a cooling rack by putting each cookie in between the cooling rack bars.
3. Microwave for the 30s at a time; keep stirring in between until it has melted completely.
4. Then put the melted bark in a sandwich baggie & snip a little bit off one corner to create a hole.
5. Squeeze melted bark over the cookie's top arc, then gently tape the bottom of the cookie against a flat surface to make the melted candy begin to ooze down the cookie. Shift it from side-to-side to create uneven edges on the bottom of the Ghost.
6. Let the almond bark dry, then pipe on eyes by melting chopped chocolate, adding it to a sandwich baggie, and cutting a hole in one corner.

7. Pipe 3 circles on each ghost cookie, two eyes, and a mouth.
8. Let it dry completely, then store in an airtight container until ready to serve.

Towering Haunted House Cake

This particular recipe yields thirty servings with a preparation time of five hours
Recipe

For the Cake (Make Twice):
1. 1 3/4 cups of all-purpose spooned flour & leveled
2. Two cups of granulated sugar
3. Two tablespoons of baking soda.
4. Half tablespoon of baking powder.
5. ¾ cup of unsweetened cocoa powder.

6. One tablespoon of kosher salt.
7. Three large eggs.
8. One cup of warm milk.
9. One teaspoon of pure vanilla extract.

2/3 cup of vegetable oil.

For Vanilla Buttercream and Decoration:

1. Two and a half cups of unsalted butter at room temperature.
2. Pinch kosher salt.
3. One and a half teaspoon of pure vanilla extract.
4. Black food coloring.
5. Seventeen chocolate sandwich cookies, divided and crushed.
6. One cup of black candy melts.
7. Silver luster dust.
8. Black and white fondant
9. 7 ½ cups of sifted confectioner's sugar.

Wilton bones & skulls sprinkle for the use of windows and doors.

Green sprinkles for moss

Green licorice or sour strings for plants

Black & gunmetal dragées for above windows & door & along with house corners

Silver & white lollipops for door trim

Black & Gray Sixlets for roof & balcony

Procedures

1. **To Make the Cake:** gently preheat the oven to 350°F. Then apply to grease a 9- by 13-inch pan & line the bottom with parchment paper. Grease the parchment.
2. Whisk altogether flour, cocoa, sugar, baking powder, baking soda, and salt with an electric mixer on medium speed till combined, about one minute.
3. Then add vanilla, oil, eggs, and milk.
4. Whisk on medium-low until it becomes smooth, about one minute. Then increase speed to medium & beat for two minutes.
5. Gently Spread batter into a prepared clean pan. Bake and rotating once till a toothpick injected in the center comes

out clean. This process will take up to forty minutes.
6. Then Cool in pan on a wire rack for fifteen minutes. Turn out onto wire rack then right side up & cold totally. Brand a second cake. Wrap cooled cakes in plastic wrap & chill for one hour & up to two days.
7. **To make the buttercream:** Beat the butter with an electric mixer on medium speed till it becomes smooth & creamy. This process will take up to one minute. Beat in the confectioners' sugar, a half cup at a time, mixing well & scraping down sides of bowl frequently.
8. Beat in salt and vanilla. [Use within two hours or refrigerate for up to one week. Before usage, bring to room temperature & beat until smooth.]
9. Move 1 2/3 cups of buttercream to a separate clean bowl, stir in ten crushed cookies. Color remaining buttercream

gray with black food colouring transfer one cup to a zip-top bag & snip a tiny hole in one corner.

Set the <u>fence template</u> on a clean baking sheet; top it up with parchment paper. Then melt black candy melts per package instruction; move it to a zip-top bag & snip a tiny hole in one corner.

Pipe melted candy on to parchment, following the template, and allow to chill.

Gently cut cake according to <u>the template</u>. Place one base layer on a clean platter, then frost top with about 2/3 cup cookie buttercream. Kindly repeat with the remaining base layer, frosting only the left- hand side. Then place a second-story layer on frosting, frost top with about 1/3 cup frosting; top up with remaining second story layer. Gently place tower pieces next to the second story, frosting up between the layers. Top up with roof pieces, frosting between the layers. Frost the exterior with gray buttercream. Then use a cake comb to create siding texture.

Then roll black fondant to around 1/8-inch thickness. Through <u>templates</u>, cut windows & door, then gently press a butter knife onto the windows to produce panes. Slightly brush windows & door lightly with luster dust and attach to the house. Roll together some black & white fondant & style minor marbled stones for the use of walkway.

Applying the gray frosting in the piping bag as glue, proceed to decorate the windows, roof, and all outside with the candies.

Then add the Chocolate Fence. Use the remaining seven crushed cookies to produce a path.

Something-To-Hide Devil's Food Cupcakes

This particular recipe will yield 12 servings, and the preparation time is 1 hour; altogether, the total time is 2 hours.

Recipe:
1. ¼ Cup of unsweetened cocoa powder.
2. One cup of sugar.
3. ¼ Teaspoon of baking soda
4. ½ Teaspoon of baking powder.
5. ½ Teaspoon of kosher salt.
6. Six tablespoons of strong coffee.
7. Yellow food coloring.

8. Cream cheese buttercream.
9. Two large eggs at room temperature.
10. One teaspoon of pure vanilla extract.
11. ½ Cup of sour cream at room temperature.
12. ½ Cup of unsalted butter at room temperature.
13. One cup of blue and yellow chocolate candies
14. 1 ¼ cup of all-purpose flour, leveled and spooned.

Procedures

1. Preheat the oven to 350°F. and line up a 12-cup standard muffin tin with clean paper liners.
2. Gently stir together cocoa & coffee until it becomes smooth, and allow to cool. Whisk salt, flour, baking soda, and baking powder in a clean bowl altogether.
3. Beat sugar & butter on medium speed with an electric mixer until light & fluffy, make up to four minutes. Then

add eggs, one at a time, beating until blended after each accumulation. Beat in vanilla.

4. Reduce mixer speed to low, & beat in flour mixture & sour cream, consecutively, beginning & ending with flour mixture, just until flour is merged. Beat in cocoa mix.

5. Spoon batter into the clean, prepared tin, separating evenly. Bake till a toothpick injected in the middle comes out clean, up to twenty-six minutes. Cool off entirely in the clean tin on a wire rack.

6. Make use of a tablespoon measure to scoop out a nice hole in the top of each cupcake. Then fill with candies, dividing evenly.

7. Tint the <u>Cream Cheese Buttercream</u> to the desired shade with good food coloring, & frost cupcakes.

8. Decorate it with additional candies.

Licorice-Eared Mice Mini-Cakes

This particular recipe will yield six servings

Recipe
1. Black licorice.
2. Black food coloring.
3. Half cup of pumpkin pie filling.
4. One box of betty crocker super moist german chocolate cake mix.
5. A cup of grade-a dark maple syrup.
6. One tub of duncan hines classic vanilla frosting.

Procedures:

1. Gently coat a mini-egg cake pan with cooking spray & fill each of the compartment to the top with prepared cake mix.
2. Then bake at 350°F for up to twenty minutes, then cool the cakes on a wire rack. Repeat the process until you've baked sixteen cakes.
3. Slowly add the black food coloring to a 3/4 tub of frosting, while stirring, until frosting turns to pale gray.
4. Microwave for ten seconds, stir it; repeat the process until frosting becomes thin enough to pour, and then coat the cakes.
5. Gently apply licorice pieces to form tails (cut to four inches) & shaped ears (cut into two and a half inches), as shown above.
6. Slowly add the black food coloring to the remaining frosting, while stirring, until frosting turns dark black.

7. Gently pour inside a freezer bag with one tip snipped off to create a piping sleeve. Make use of the piping sleeve to draw the eyes, nose, & whiskers.

Spiced Chocolate Bat Cookies

These spicy chocolate cookies are the perfect fit for a spooky Halloween treat. It yields one dozen, and preparation time is forty-five minutes, and the total time is two hours, thirty minutes.

Recipes:
1. Two and a half cups of flour.
2. Half teaspoon of ground cardamom.
3. Half teaspoon of ground cinnamon.
4. Half teaspoon of baking powder.
5. Half teaspoon of baking soda.
6. ¾ Cup of dark brown sugar.
7. Half teaspoon of fine sea salt.

8. Half a cup of dark chocolate powder.
9. One large egg
10. One and a half stick unsalted butter.
11. Granulated sugar.
12. Silver edible sugar pearls.
13. Half cup of unsulphured molasses.

Procedures:

1. In a large clean bowl, gently whisk together the first seven ingredients until well joined and set aside.
2. Place sugar & butter in a large clean bowl and beat using the paddle attachment of an electric mixer.
3. Add Egg & beat until pale and fluffy, about four minutes. Add molasses, & mix to combine. Add flour mixture & beat until just combined, about one minute.
4. Divide the dough in half. Place each between 2 pieces of clean parchment paper, and roll to a 3/8-inch-thick disk. Refrigerate for one hour.

5. Heat the oven to 325 0 F. Dust the countertop with cocoa powder.
6. Move dough to countertop & cut cookie shaped with a 6-inch bat-shaped cutter or favorite size (adjust the baking time accordingly).
7. Replicate with remaining dough & place one inch apart on clean parchment paper-lined baking sheets.
8. Bake about twelve minutes, rotating the baking sheets halfway through baking, until cookies are well crisp. Slightly press two sugar pearls into each cookie for creation eyes. Let cookies cool for five minutes on baking sheets & transfer to a wire rack to cool off completely.
9. Make use of a subtle pastry brush to lightly coat the tops of the bat wings with water. Sprinkle it with sugar & allow to set.

Peanut Butter Acorns

A small peanut butter cookie & a chocolate kiss in the form of an acorn make a tasty and festive fall dessert. It yields one dozen, and preparation time is fifteen minutes, cook time is ten minutes, and the total time is thirty-five minutes.

Recipes:
1. 3/4 cup of smooth, natural peanut butter.
2. 3/4 cup of sugar.
3. One teaspoon of vanilla.
4. One large egg.
5. One tablespoon of flour.
6. 1/2 cup of mini chocolate chips.
7. 48 chocolate kisses

Procedures:
1. Gently heat the oven to 350 o F.
2. Beat the first five ingredients in a bowl using an electric mixer until it is well joined.
3. Then spoon dough by rounded 1/4 teaspoonfuls onto a clean, unlined baking sheet. Then flatten each piece into a dome shape.
4. Bake about ten minutes or until golden around each edge; keep rotating baking sheet halfway through baking.
5. Allow to cool off for five minutes on the baking sheets.
6. Microwave the 1/4 cup mini chips in a small heat-proof bowl on high for thirty seconds, stirring at ten-second intervals.
7. Dip the bottom end of each chocolate kiss in melted chocolate & place on the flat side of each cookie. Use the same technique to fix a mini chip "stem" to

the top of each cookie in completing the acorn.

Spooky Fingers

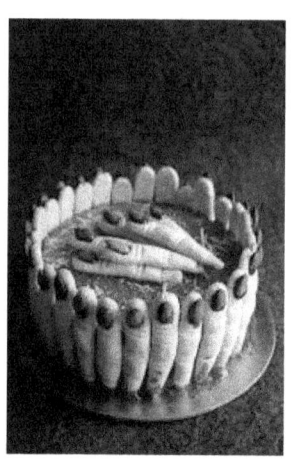

Delicious chocolate dipped pretzels are Halloween ready with the necessary addition of pumpkin seeds.

This recipe yields one dozen, and preparation time is ten minutes. And the total time is fifteen minutes.

Recipes:
1. Eight ounces of white chocolate.
2. 20 pretzel rods.
3. 20 pepitas (pumpkin seeds)

Procedures:

1. Line cookie sheet with clean waxed paper. Place the chocolate in a large neat microwave-safe bowl. Microwave on high in thirty seconds increments till almost melted, occasionally stirring up until smooth.
2. Holding one pretzel rod at a time over melted chocolate and spoon some chocolate over pretzel to coat, leaving about three inches uncoated at one end. Calmly place on prepared cookie sheet. Instantly press 1 pepita onto coated tip to look like a fingernail. Repeat this step with the remaining ingredients. Refrigerate for fifteen minutes to set chocolate. Fingers could be kept at room temperature in an airtight container for up to two weeks.

Banana Mummies

These beautifully spooky banana mummies will be the sensation hit of any Halloween party treat table. It yields 8 servings and 25 mins preparation time, and the total time for preparing is 25 mins.

Recipes:
1. Four bananas.
2. One-pound white chocolate.
3. 4 ounces of white chocolate.
4. 16 mini m&m's
5. 4 oz. Milk chocolate chips
6. 8 lollipop sticks

Procedures:
1. Line up a large baking sheet with a clean bakery paper.
2. Lance each banana half with a lollipop stick & freeze until firm, at least for two hours.
3. According to package instructions, in a large microwave-safe measuring cup, melt one- pound of white chocolate in the microwave.
4. One at a time gently dips the bananas into the chocolate to properly coat, shaking off excess, if any. Return to the baking sheet & immediately place two M&M candies near the top for making the eyes.
5. Then melt the remaining white chocolate in the microwave according to package instructions & fill a small piping bag fitted with a small, round nozzle tip.

6. Pipe the zigzags over the banana to form bandages. Duplicate this step with the use of milk chocolate, if using. Chill until ready to serve.

Pumpkin Rice Krispies Treats

This recipe takes up to 20 minutes for preparation, and it yields 6 servings, cook time is 5 minutes, and ready in 25 minutes.

Recipes:
1. six cups of rice Krispies cereal.
2. 3 Tablespoon of salted butter
3. 10 ounces of mini marshmallows
4. Orange gel food coloring.

5. Three pretzel rods, end portions broken off into 2-inch pieces (so you'll have 6 pieces)
6. six mini green airheads or green fondant
7. Non-stick cooking spray.

Procedures:
1. Measure out rice Krispies cereal & pour it into a clean bowl.
2. Melt the butter in a 4-quart non-stick clean saucepan over medium-low heat.
3. Then add marshmallows and stir, and as they begin to melt, start adding in the gel food coloring till your desired color is achieved.
4. Then Stir constantly until the marshmallows have melted.
5. Gently remove from heat, then immediately pour in the Rice Krispies cereal & gently stir & fold with a spatula until cereal is evenly coated.

6. Let mixture cool slightly until it's cool enough to handle with your bare hands.
7. Then spray hands with non-stick cooking spray, then shape rice Krispie treats mixture into small balls about the size of a baseball, then insert one piece of the pretzel rod into the top center & reshape the pumpkin as desirable.
8. Transfer to a clean dish sprayed lightly with cooking spray.
9. Starting on one side of the airhead, candy gently cut out a leaf shape with clean scissors then use the remaining part of the piece of candy to roll & shape into a well-organized thin rope shape, then twist into a vine shape or just shape the fondant, therefore, no cutting required.

Gently place candy on the sides of each pretzel on the pumpkin.

Replicate with remaining candy & Store in an airtight container.

Candy Corn Chocolate Chip Cookie Cake

Recipes:

1. 3/4 cup of salted butter at room temperature
2. Half cup brown sugar, which is lightly packed
3. Half cup of sugar
4. One Egg
5. One teaspoon of vanilla extract
6. 1 1/4 cups of all-purpose flour
7. Half cup of cocoa (I made use of Hershey's Special Dark)
8. One teaspoon of baking soda
9. 1/2 –3/4 cup of chocolate chunks or chocolate chips

10. 1/2 –3/4 cup of candy corn

Recipe for chocolate icing:
1. 1/4 cup of butter
2. 1/4 cup of shortening
3. Two cups of powdered sugar
4. Half teaspoon of vanilla
5. 1/4 cup of cocoa
6. Two tablespoons of water or milk.

Procedures:

For chocolate cookie cake:

1. Preheat the oven to 350 degrees & prepare on an inch cake pan by putting the parchment paper in the bottom of the pan & spraying the sides with a non-stick spray.

2. Cream butter & sugars together until light and fluffy, up till four minutes.

3. Mix in vanilla extract and Egg.

4. Add cocoa, flour & baking soda & mix until combined.

5. Stir well in chocolate chunks & candy corn.

6. The dough will be thick & sticky.

7. Spread well the dough evenly into the cake pan.

8. Bake well for up to twenty minutes. The middle may still look a little underdone, but it will firm up & continue cooking as it cools.

9. Gently remove from oven & let cool completely in pan, then carefully remove it.

For the chocolate icing:

1. Beat the shortening & butter until it becomes smooth.

2. Then add vanilla, cocoa & half of powdered sugar.

3. Mix well until combined.

4. Add 1-2 tablespoons of water.

5. Then add the rest of the powdered sugar & mix until smooth.

6. Proceed to add water to get the right steadiness.

Spooky Halloween Pretzels

Recipes:

1. 16 ounces of milk or semisweet melted chocolate.
2. 8 ounces of high quality melted white chocolate.
3. 16 pretzel twists [large]
4. 8 pretzel rods
5. Oreos, melted chocolate, candy eyes, chocolate candy melts, melted white chocolate, black licorice, fall M&M's

Procedures:

For spooky owls:

1. Dip each of the pretzel twists in melted chocolate & place on a clean parchment-lined baking sheet.
2. Split an Oreo in half & use for the eyes. Place the pretzels in the refrigerator to set for ten minutes.
3. Once the chocolate is ready, add a little dot of melted chocolate to the middle of each Oreo & attach the candy eyes.
4. Drizzle a line of the readily made chocolate above the eyebrows' eyes and attach two pieces of licorice to each eye. Mark a small amount of chocolate between the Oreos & insert an M & M to produce a nose if you wish.
5. Sprinkle the owl lightly with grey or black sanding sugar.
6. Place back in the freezer for ten minutes to set. The owls can be created with both chocolate & white chocolate enclosed pretzel twists.

For spooky Ghost:

1. Kindly dip each pretzel twist in melted white chocolate & place on a parchment-lined baking sheet.

2. Then insert 2 chocolate candy melts to create the eyes and place the pretzels in the freezer to set for ten minutes.

For spooky mummies:

1. Gently dip each pretzel twist in melted white chocolate & place on a clean parchment-lined baking sheet.

2. Then fill in the 3 pretzel holes by drizzling melted white chocolate inside. Then insert two candy eyes.

3. Proceed to place the pretzels in the freezer to set for up to ten minutes.

For spooky wands:

1. Gently dip each pretzel rod in chocolate & return to the parchment-lined baking sheets.

2. Gently Place the pretzels in the freezer to set for up to ten minutes.

3. Once this is set, drizzle melted chocolate up & down the pretzel rods &

then sprinkles with gold stars. Freeze for ten minutes to set.

Haunted Haystacks

Recipes:

1. One cup butterscotch chips
2. 1/4 cup creamy peanut butter

3. Two cups chow mein noodles
4. 3/4 cup mini marshmallows
5. candy eyeballs

   Procedures:

1. Melt butterscotch chips in the microwave for approximately one minute to one minute thirty seconds. Stir slowly until it smoothens, then add some peanut butter, stirring once again.

2. Add into the chow mein noodles & marshmallows & stir to coat.

3. Drop by rounded tablespoonfuls onto wax paper. Carefully arrange the candy eyeballs on one side of each treat. Then let it cool to set. You can store leftovers in an air-free container.

4. For the purple, white, and green Haunted Haystacks, melt 1/3 cup candy melts in a glass bowl (about thirty - sixty seconds in the microwave), then add half cup chow mein noodles. Stir to

coat, drop by rounded tablespoonfuls onto wax paper. Gently arrange candy eyeballs on each treat, then let cool to set.

Candy Corn White Chocolate M&M Blondies

Recipes:
1. Half cup of melted unsalted butter.
2. One large Egg
3. One cup of light brown sugar[packed]
4. One tablespoon of vanilla extract
5. One cup of all-purpose flour
6. 9.9 ounces of a bag of M&Ms Candy Corn White Chocolate Candies

Procedures:

1. Gently preheat the oven to 350F. Then line an 8-by-8-inch baking pan with clean aluminum foil, spray with cooking spray, and set aside.
2. In a large microwave-safe bowl, slowly melt the butter, about one minute on high power.
3. Wait temporarily before adding the Egg, so you don't get it scrambled.
4. Then add the vanilla, Egg, brown sugar, & whisk until it becomes smooth.
5. Add the flour & stir until just combined, don't overmix it.
6. Stir in one cup of M&Ms

7. Turn batter out into a clean, prepared pan, smoothing the top part lightly with a spatula.
8. Then add the remaining M&Ms to top of the batter, scattering them evenly & pressing them down lightly with your clean finger.

9. Bake for about twenty-three minutes, or until it's done. At twenty-three minutes, they're very soft & moist. If you prefer firmer & dryer bars, bake for a few minutes longer if favored.

10. A clean toothpick inserted in the center should come out clean, or maybe with a few moist crumbs, but no batter. Allow bars to cool in the pan for at least thirty minutes before slicing & serving.

11. Bars will keep airtight at room temperature for up to one week or in the freezer for up to six months.

Halloween Pumpkin Cookie Cake

This particular recipe will take up to 20 minutes for preparation, and cook time is 25 minutes with 45 minutes, and it yields 8-10 servings.

Recipes:
1. One box of Krusteaz Pumpkin Spice Cookie Mix
2. Half cup butter as called for on the box.
3. One large Egg is called for on the box.
4. Four teaspoons of water for the icing
5. Black food coloring
6. Halloween sprinkles

Procedures:

1. Preheat the griddle to 350°F and Line an eight or 9-inches round pan with foil & spray with a non-stick cooking spray.

2. Mix the cookie mix with the butter & Egg until a thick cookie dough is formed. Press it into the prepared pan.

3. Bake for up to 30 minutes, or until it becomes brown around the edges & no longer shiny on top. Cool completely before you start frosting.

4. Whisk icing packet & water until icing forms desired steadiness.

5. Then add 4-6 drops of black food coloring & stir to distribute color. Frost the cookie cake & then top with Halloween sprinkles.

Halloween Sprinkle Cookies

Recipes:
1. Three cups of all-purpose flour
2. One teaspoon of baking powder
3. Half teaspoon of salt
4. One cup unsalted butter
5. One cup of sugar
6. One Egg
7. One and a half teaspoons vanilla extract
8. 3-4 tablespoons of sprinkles [your choice]

Procedures:
1. In a large clean bowl, gently add flour and baking powder & salt. Gently Whisk together & set aside.

2. In the bowl of an electric mixer, proceed to add butter & beat until it becomes smooth.
3. Add sugar & blend until thoroughly combined & fluffy.
4. Add vanilla & Egg and blend.
5. While mixing, gradually pour in the bowl of flour.
6. Mix until dough forms & start drawing away from the sides of the bowl.
7. Add two tablespoons sprinkles & blend just until merged.
8. Gently scoop the dough out onto a work surface & form into two large balls. Avoid working the dough with your bare hands too much, as this may result in the colors of the sprinkles to bleed.
9. Gently lay a large piece of plastic wrap on your work surface. Place a dough ball on top & press the dough down just a bit to flatten the shape. Top the dough with another sheet of plastic

wrap, then roll out the dough between the two sheets. This method eradicates the need for adding extra flour.

Once the dough is your favorite thickness (around 1/3 of an inch), gently remove the top layer of plastic wrap & sprinkle the dough's whole top surface with sprinkles.

Carefully roll your rolling pin over the sprinkle covered dough to surround the sprinkles into the dough.

 Cut out cookies as preferred. I made use of a large knife to cut the dough into 1x4-inches strips.

Gently place similar sized cookies together at least half-inch apart on a baking sheet lined with clean parchment paper or a Silpat type liner.

Place the whole baking sheet of unbaked cookies in the fridge for fifteen minutes or freezer for at least five minutes. This step will help to prevent spreading.

Bake up to ten minutes in a preheated 350*F oven.

Cool on the baking sheet for up to two minutes, and then proceed to a cooling rack.

Once it is thoroughly cooled, preserve the cookies in a sealed container. The baked cookies will keep on being fresh when preserved well for at least one week.

Halloween Chocolate Chip Cookies

Recipes:
1. 2 1/4 cups of all-purpose flour
2. One teaspoon of baking soda
3. One teaspoon of salt
4. A cup of unsalted butter.
5. Half cup of sugar
6. One cup of packed light brown sugar
7. One & a half teaspoons of vanilla extract
8. Two large eggs
9. Two cups of semisweet chocolate chips, plus more for topping

Chocolate candy melts

Candy eyes

Procedures:

1. In a clean medium bowl, whisk together the baking soda, flour, and salt. Then set the mixture aside.
2. In the big bowl of a stand mixer fitted with the paddle attachment, cream together the butter, sugar, brown sugar & vanilla extract until light & fluffy, scraping down the sides as desired.
3. Gently add the eggs, beating between each addition, then add the flour mixture & beat just until united.
4. Add the chocolate chips & beat until incorporated, then cover & refrigerate the dough for a minimum of two hours & up to overnight.
5. Proceed to Preheat the oven to 375°F & line 2 baking sheets with Silpat baking mats or parchment paper.
6. Using two spoons or an ice cream scoop, share out about two tablespoons of the dough into mounds, spacing the mounds at least two inches apart.

7. Add two or three additional chocolate chips to the tops of the cookies. These will make be the spider "bodies."
8. Gently bake the cookies for up to eleven minutes or until they are set around the edges but still slightly underbaked in the centers. Remove the cookies from the oven & allow them to cool on the baking sheet for five minutes before transferring them to a rack to cool off completely.
9. Once the cookies have adequately cooled, melt the chocolate candy melts per the package directions, then transfer the chocolate to a sealable plastic bag or piping bag.

Trim off the tip, then pipe spider "legs" coming out of the chocolate chips on the tops of the cookies. Assign the spider "eyes" by accumulating two chocolate dots above the chocolate chips at that point, attaching the candy eyes. Allow the chocolate to set, then serve.

Pumpkin Pretzels With Jack-O-Lantern Faces For Halloween

Recipes:
1. 12 ounces Orange Candy Melts, melted
2. 65 Pretzel Dipping Sticks
3. 2 ounces Green Candy Melts, melted
4. 4 ounces Black Candy Melts, melted

Procedures:
1. Kindly dip one pretzel into the orange candy melts & coat it thoroughly.
2. Gently remove from the candy using a dipping fork & allow excess to drip off.
3. Set pretzel on a clean parchment paper-lined baking sheet.
4. Then dip a second pretzel & set it right next to the first pretzel.

5. Proceed to repeat until you have a row of 6 candy-coated pretzels lined up, forming a rectangle pumpkin.
6. Freeze for about three minutes, just until the candy coating gets hard.
7. Repeat creating a total of ten pretzel pumpkins. You should have five extra pretzels.
8. Break about half-inch off each end of the remaining pretzels.
9. Assign one small pretzel piece to each of the pumpkins to make the stem.
10. Pour the melted green candy melts into a zip-top bag or squeeze bottle.
11. Pipe on some green leaves & a vine is going down one side of each of the pumpkin.
12. Pour the black candy melts into another bag or bottle.
13. Pipe 2 triangle eyes, 1 triangle nose, and 1 toothy grin onto each pretzel pumpkin to make them look like jack-o-lanterns.

14. Then chill for about 1 minute just until the decorations strengthen.

Recipe Proceedings:
- Do not allow to chill for too long, or the candy coating on your pretzels might crack.
- If you choose to dip your pretzels in pure white chocolate, you will need to melt & temper the chocolate, then apply color using an oil-based orange candy coloring.
- Then allow the white chocolate dipped pretzels to properly chill in the refrigerator, not the freezer, for about five minutes just until the chocolate gets hardens.

Chocolate Monster Halloween Cookies

Recipes:
For the cookies;
1. Two cups of plain (all-purp) flour.
2. Half cup of dutch processed cocoa.
3. Half teaspoon of baking powder.
4. ¾ cup of white sugar.
5. Half cup of unsalted butter, cold & cut into cubes.
6. One large cold Egg
7. One teaspoon of vanilla extract.
8. One tablespoon of cold milk.

For the vanilla buttercream filling;
1. One and a half cups of powdered icing sugar.

2. Eighty grams of softened stick unsalted butter.
3. Two teaspoons of thickened heavy cream.
4. A pinch of salt
5. One teaspoon of vanilla extract.
6. Orange and purple food coloring.
7. Sprinkles & monster eye candies for decorating.

Procedures:
For cookies
1. Preheat the oven to 350F fan-forced and line two baking trays with baking paper.
2. Then add the baking powder, flour, sugar, and cocoa to the processor & process to combine.
3. Add the cold butter & process again for another thirty seconds until it is finely chopped through the flour

combination. It may still be a little lumpy, and that's okay.
4. Lastly, add the Egg, vanilla & half of the milk. Process again for about forty seconds until everything is well joined & the dough starts forming large clumps. If it's not entirely sticking together, & the rest of the milk & set-to again.
5. Proceed to tip the mix out onto a clean surface & pull together with your hands, kneading lightly until it starts to stay together only one minute or so.
6. Then layout a long sheet of baking paper & lay the dough in the center of one half of it.
7. Fold the other half over the top &make use of a rolling pin to roll the dough out to approximately 4-5mm thick. Every so often, peel the paper away, then recover (top first, then flip it over to do the bottom) - this will halt any

crumples in the paper producing indentations in the cookies.
8. Place in the fridge for up to thirty minutes before moving on.
9. Make use of a 2-inch circle cutter to cut as many cookies as you can. Transfer them to a baking tray carefully about one inch apart. Re-roll the dough & repeat until it has all been used.

Bake in the oven for six minutes, turn the trays, bake for another six minutes. Move them to a wire rack & allow to cool completely.

For the vanilla buttercream filling
1. Give the processor bowl a quick rinse, then proceeds to add the sugar, cream, butter, vanilla & salt. Process the whole lot for about three minutes on the low setting until smooth & pale.
2. Divide the buttercream between 2 bowls, then color one with orange & one with purple coloring.

3. Place a teaspoon of buttercream on half of the cookies so that it sits just a little off the center. Press another cookie down on the top at an angle.

4. Proceed to add the eyes & sprinkles if using them. If the buttercream needs to firm up, place the cookies in the fridge, or otherwise serve straight away.

Notes:

1. For best results, you must always weigh ingredients like sugar and flour.

2. [Kitchen scales like these](#) are relatively cheap, but if you can't weigh the ingredients, you can use the spoon & level method (avoid scooping).

3. I made use of a standard Australian 20ml tbsp (4 teaspoons worldwide).

Spider Oreo Balls

Recipes:
1. One package of OREO Cookies divided (8 ounces)
2. One package of full-fat cream cheese at room temperature (8 ounces)
3. 2 & 2/3rds cup chocolate chips I like milk chocolate best
4. 3-4 teaspoons vegetable oil

5. Spider Decoration
6. 96 Candy eyeballs
7. 1/3 cup of brown sprinkles
8. Thin black licorice

Procedures:

1. Place in a large blender or food processor, process the OREO's up until they resemble crumbs.
2. Beat together the room temperature cream cheese & cookie crumbs up until blended.
3. Shape the mixture into 48 balls & then freeze the balls for 10 minutes.
4. In a microwave-safe bowl, combine the chocolate chips & vegetable oil. (I prefer to separate the chocolate and do up to three batches, so it stays pleasant & melted while dipping the cookie balls in).
5. Microwave in bursts of twenty seconds, stirring for fifteen seconds in between each burst up until the chocolate is fully melted.

6. Gently dip the balls in the melted chocolate, then add more vegetable oil to thin the chocolate if needed & place on a tray lined with a clean parchment paper.
7. Before it dries up, sprinkle the top of the balls with brown sprinkles & then press 2 candy eyes onto each ball.
8. Cut the licorice with scissors & press into the cookie ball. Ensure you do this before the chocolate has a chance to harden. It's helpful to insert two legs, one on each side at a time, to get leverage to press the legs in fully.
9. Proceed to allow the chocolate to harden & dry.

Boo-Nilla Ghost Milkshakes

Recipes
Ingredients for Milk-shake
1. Four cups vanilla bean ice cream
2. 1/2-1 3/4 cup whole milk
3. two teaspoon vanilla extract

Topping
1. 1 cup heavy cream
2. 3 tablespoon powdered sugar
3. 1/2 teaspoon vanilla extract

HALLOWEEN SNAGGLE-TOOTH FRUIT TREATS

INGREDIENTS:

☐ 4 cored, quartered apples, Honeycrisp
☐ 1 x 2 1/4oz. pkg. of blanched almonds, slivered

DIRECTIONS:

Step 1

With sharp, small knife, cut lengthways wedge from skin side of apple quarters. Leave peel around wedges for lips.

Step 2

Poke five or six almond slivers in tops and bottoms of cut-out areas, making snaggle teeth. Serve.

Halloween Deviled Eggs

INGREDIENTS:

- 1/2 cup of soy sauce, dark
- 7 cups of water, filtered
- 2 tbsp. of oil, chili
- 2 tbsp. of tea leaves, black, loose (tea bags can be cut open if you like)
- 1 tbsp. of Chinese 5 spice powder blend
- 2 tsp. of salt, kosher + extra, as desired
- Pepper, ground, as desired
- 1 tsp. of sugar, granulated
- 12 eggs, large
- 4 tbsp. of mayonnaise, reduced fat
- 1 tbsp. of mustard, yellow
- 2 tsp. of sauce, sriracha
- Food coloring gel, orange

☐ To garnish: sesame seeds, black

DIRECTIONS:

Step 1

In large pan, bring filtered water, sugar, kosher salt, 5-spice powder blend, tea leaves, chili oil and soy sauce to boil.

Step 2

Reduce heat and cover pan. Simmer for 10-12 minutes. Remove pan from heat. Remove lid and allow to cool.

Step 3

Hard boil eggs. Chill them immediately in iced water. Crack shells. Submerge eggs completely in tea and sauce mixture. Place in refrigerator for a full day. **Step 4**

Peel eggs. Cut thin slivers of whites from wider end of eggs so they will stand. Slice tops off eggs. Remove yolks to medium bowl.

Step 5

Mash yolks with mustard, mayo and sriracha. Season as desired. Add food coloring. Mix well. **Step 6**

Pipe yolk and seasoning mixture into empty egg whites. Use sesame seeds to garnish. Serve.

Witch's Kid-Friendly Halloween Brew

INGREDIENTS:
☐ 1 x 10oz. pkg. of frozen, sweetened raspberries 2 1/2 cups of cocktail, cranberry juice ☐ 2 envelopes of unsweetened gelatin ☐ 2 liters of ginger ale ☐ 2 litersof non-alcoholic apple cider, sparkling 6 gummy snakes, candy

DIRECTIONS:
Step 1

To prepare frozen, fake hand, wash and rinse outside of rubber glove. Turn the glove inside out. Set it aside.

Step 2

In four-cup measuring cup, mix cranberry juice with thawed raspberries.

Step 3

Pour two cups of raspberry mixture in small pan. Sprinkle gelatin atop the mixture. Allow it to stand for two minutes.

Step 4

Warm the mixture on low heat, constantly stirring, till gelatin dissolves. Mix this back in with raspberry mixture in measuring cup.

Step 5

Pour the raspberry mixture in glove. Gather top of glove and securely tie. Freeze till solid. You can freeze it for a few days, if you have the time.

Step 6

When preparing to serve, cut glove carefully away from the frozen raspberry hand. Place it with palm side facing up and lean against side of punch bowl. Add cider and ginger ale. Use gummy snakes to garnish. Serve.

Scary Butternut Squash Spider Web Soup

INGREDIENTS:
For the soup
☐ 3 cups of chicken broth, low sodium
☐ 4 cups of peeled, cubed squash, butternut
☐ 1 tsp. of oil, coconut
☐ 1 chopped onion, medium
☐ 1 cup of chopped carrots

- [ ] 2/3 cup of coconut milk, canned
- [ ] 3/4 tsp. of curry pwder, mild

For spider web
- [ ] 2 1/2 tbsp. of coconut milk, canned
- [ ] 1 cup of Greek yogurt, fatfree, plain

DIRECTIONS:

Step 1

Heat a large pot on med. heat till hot. Add the coconut oil, carrots and onions. Sauté till veggies soften.

Step 2

Add squash and broth. Cover pot. Bring to boil. Remove the lid. Allow to simmer till squash becomes tender. Add the curry powder.

Step 3

Puree batches of soup in food processor. Return to the pot.

Step 4

Add and stir in 2/3 cup of coconut milk. Heat through. Ladle soup into bowls and drizzle the yogurt mixture in lines on top of soup, so it looks like spider webs. Serve.

Classic Dirt Cake

Makes 10 +/- Servings
INGREDIENTS:
- [ ] 1/2 cup salted butter
- [ ] 1 x 8oz. pkg. of cream cheese
- [ ] 1/2 cup of powdered sugar
- [ ] 2 x 3 1/2oz. pkgs. of vanilla instant pudding mix 3 1/2 cups of milk, 2%

- [ ] 1 x 12oz. container of frozen whipped topping 32 oz. of chocolate sandwich cookies with cream filling

DIRECTIONS:

Step 1

In a food processor, chop the cookies very finely. White cream should disappear when done.

Step 2

Mix the butter, sugar and cream cheese in medium bowl.

Step 3

In larger bowl, mix the milk, whipped topping and pudding together.

Step 4

Combine the pudding mixture with cream mixture and mix well.

Step 5

Starting with the cookies and then the cream mixture, layer back and forth, repeating the layers. Chill till you are ready for serving. Add artificial flowers. Serve.

Melted Mud Chocolate

Preparation time:

20 minutes
Yield: 3 servings

INGREDIENTS:
- [ ] 1 cup dark chocolate
- [ ] 1 cup milk
- [ ] 2 tablespoons caster sugar
- [ ] 1 tablespoon butter
- [ ] 2 tablespoons cocoa powder
- [ ] 2 tablespoons chocolate syrup

DIRECTIONS
Step 1

Melt butter in pan, add chocolate and stir till the chocolate is melted. **Step 2** Add milk, sugar, chocolate syrup, cocoa powder and mix well. **Step 3** Transfer to serving bowls and serve. **Step 4** Enjoy.

Spooky Spider Cookies

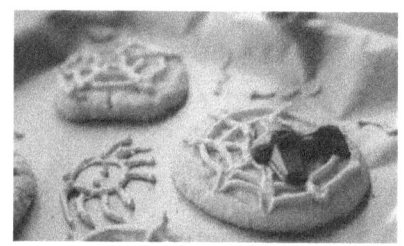

Preparation time: 20 minutes
Yield: 6 servings

INGREDIENTS:
- 1 cup all-purpose flour
- 1 cup chocolate, melted
- ½ cup peanut butter
- ½ cup caster sugar
- 1 egg
- ¼ teaspoon baking powder
- Candy eyes, as much required
- Chocolate truffles, as much needed

DIRECTIONS

Step 1

Preheat oven at 355 degrees.

Step 2
In a bowl beat egg with sugar.

Step 3
Add baking powder, peanut butter, flour and mix well.

Step 4
Make round balls with this mixture and make a small cavity on it by pressing lightly with finger.

Step 5
Place into greased baking dish and bake for 15-20 minutes.

Step 6
Now place truffle on cookies, make legs with chocolate and place eyes.

Step 7
Enjoy.

Evil Spirit Pops

Preparation time: 10 minutes
Yield: 10 servings

INGREDIENTS:
- ½ oz. cup marshmallows
- ¼ cup white chocolate, melted
- 10 toothpicks
- Edible marker

DIRECTIONS

Step 1
Insert toothpick into each marshmallow and dip into chocolate lightly. **Step 2** Place into refrigerator for 10 minutes. **Step 3** Make eyes, nose and lips with edible marker.

Step   **4**

Enjoy.

Witch Hat Cookies

Preparation time: 40 minutes
Yield: 6 servings
INGREDIENTS:
- [ ] 1 cup all-purpose flour
- [ ] 1 cup cocoa powder
- [ ] 1 cup caster sugar
- [ ] 2 tablespoons butter
- [ ] 1 egg
- [ ] ¼ cup milk
- [ ] ¼ teaspoon orange food color

☐ 2 egg whites ☐ 1 cup chocolate, melted

DIRECTIONS

Step 1

Preheat oven at 355 degrees.

Step 2

In blender add flour, cocoa powder, butter, milk, ½ cup sugar and blend well.

Step 3

Spread dough on clean surface and roll out into ¼ inch thick sheet.

Step 4

Cut with a round cutter and place into greased baking tray, bake for 30 minutes.

Step 5

Beat eggs white till fluffy, add caster and food colour, beat well. Transfer to piping bag.

Step 6

Add melted chocolate into piping bag.

Step 7

Now top each cookie with icing then pipe out chocolate on it in the form of hat.

Step 8

Place into refrigerator for 15 minutes.
Step **9**
Serve and enjoy.

Pumpkin Cheesecake Dip

INGREDIENTS:

☐ 1 x 3.4 ounce pkg. of instant pudding, pumpkin spice 3/4 cup of coffee creamer, pumpkin pie spice

☐ 1 x 8 ounce pkg. of softened cream cheese, light 1/4 cup of sugar, granulated
☐ 2 cups of frozen, thawed whipped topping
☐ For garnishing: graham cracker crumbs

DIRECTIONS:
Step **1**

In medium bowl, whisk coffee creamer and pudding together. Set the mixture aside for five to seven minutes.
Step 2

In separate medium bowl, beat cream cheese and granulated sugar together.
Step 3
Add pudding mixture to cream cheese/sugar mixture. Beat well.
Step 4
Once the mixtures have combined well, fold in whipped topping. Place in the refrigerator. **Step 5**

When you are prepared to serve the treat, fill the bowl with the dip mixture and top with the graham cracker crumbs. Serve.

Classic Dirt Cake

INGREDIENTS:

- [ ] 1/2 cup salted butter
- [ ] 1 x 8 oz. pkg. of cream cheese
- [ ] 1/2 cup of powdered sugar
- [ ] 2 x 3 1/2 oz. pkgs. of vanilla instant pudding mix 3 1/2 cups of milk, 2%

- [ ] 1 x 12 oz. container of frozen whipped topping 32 oz. of chocolate sandwich cookies with cream filling

DIRECTIONS:

Step 1

In a food processor, chop the cookies very finely. White cream should disappear when done.

Step 2

Mix the butter, sugar and cream cheese in medium bowl.

Step 3

In larger bowl, mix the milk, whipped topping and pudding together.

Step 4

Combine the pudding mixture with cream mixture and mix well.

Step 5

Starting with the cookies and then the cream mixture, layer back and forth, repeating the layers. Chill till you are ready for serving. Add artificial flowers. Serve.

Pumpkin Face Quesadillas

INGREDIENTS:
- [ ] Nonstick spray
- [ ] 2 cups of chicken, rotisserie, shredded
- [ ] 1/2 lime, fresh, juice only
- [ ] 1/2 tsp. of garlic powder
- [ ] 1/2 tsp. of chili powder
- [ ] 8 medium tortillas, flour
- [ ] 3/4 cup of cheddar cheese shreds
- [ ] 3/4 cup of Monterey Jack cheese shreds
- [ ] 1 tbsp. of oil, olive
- [ ] To serve: hot sauce, as desired

DIRECTIONS:

Step 1

Preheat the oven to 425F. Spray large

cookie sheet with non-stick spray.

Step 2

In large-sized bowl, add the chicken. Toss it with lime juice, garlic powder and chili powder.

Step 3

To assemble your quesadillas, cut jack-o-lantern patterns into four tortillas with a knife.

Step 4

Sprinkle cheese and chicken on remaining flour tortillas. Top them with the jack-o-lantern "faces".

Step 5

Next, place the quesadillas on cookie sheet. Brush them with oil. Bake in 425F oven for 12-15 minutes, till tortillas turn golden in color and the cheese becomes melty. Serve along with the hot sauce, as desired.

Pumpkin Face Quesadillas

Makes 4 Servings

INGREDIENTS:
- Nonstick spray
- 2 cups of chicken, rotisserie, shredded
- 1/2 lime, fresh, juice only
- 1/2 tsp. of garlic powder
- 1/2 tsp. of chili powder
- 8 medium tortillas, flour
- 3/4 cup of cheddar cheese shreds
- 3/4 cup of Monterey Jack cheese shreds
- 1 tbsp. of oil, olive
- To serve: hot sauce, as desired

DIRECTIONS:

Step 1

Preheat the oven to 425F. Spray large cookie sheet with non-stick spray.

Step 2

In large-sized bowl, add the chicken. Toss it with lime juice, garlic powder and chili powder.

Step 3

To assemble your quesadillas, cut jack-o-lantern patterns into four tortillas with a knife.

Step 4

Sprinkle cheese and chicken on remaining flour tortillas. Top them with the jack-o-lantern "faces".

Step 5

Next, place the quesadillas on cookie sheet. Brush them with oil. Bake in 425F oven for 12-15 minutes, till tortillas turn golden in color and the cheese becomes melty. Serve along with the hot sauce, as desired.

Halloween Pumpkin Spice Bars

Makes 24 Servings
INGREDIENTS:
- 4 eggs, large
- 1 2/3 cup of granulated sugar
- 1 cup of vegetable oil
- 1 x 15oz. can of pumpkin
- 2 cups of flour all-purpose
- 1 tsp. of baking soda
- 2 tsp. of baking powder
- 2 tsp. of ground cinnamon
- 1 tsp. of table salt
- 1 x 3oz. pkg. of cream cheese, light
- 1/2 cup of salted butter

- [ ] 1 tsp. of vanilla extract, pure
- [ ] 2 cups of powdered sugar

DIRECTIONS:

Step 1

Preheat the oven to 350F.

Step 2

To prepare frosting, cream the butter and cream cheese together. Add vanilla and stir. Add powdered sugar a bit at a time while beating till you have a smooth mixture.

Step 3

In medium mixing bowl, combine oil, sugar, pumpkin and eggs with electric mixer till fluffy and light.

Step 4

Sift together flour, baking soda, baking powder, salt and cinnamon. Stir into pumpkin mixture till combined well.

Step 5

Evenly spread batter in 15" x 10" jelly roll pan. Bake in 350F oven for 20-30 minutes. Remove from oven. Allow to cool, then frost, evenly spreading atop cooled bars. Slice in squares. Serve.

Mummy Hot Dogs

Makes 16 Servings

INGREDIENTS:

☐ 12 hot dogs regular length (not foot-longs)

☐ 1 pkg. of crescent rolls, eight

☐ Mustard, yellow

DIRECTIONS:

Step 1

Preheat the oven to 375F. Line cookie sheet with baking paper.

Step 2

Dry the hot dogs with paper towels if they're wet.

Step 3

Using pizza or pastry cutter, cut crescent roll triangles into very thin strips.

Step 4

Pull, then stretch strips and wrap them around the hot dogs. Tuck loose dough as needed, under the bottom or back of hot dogs. Leave small openings for the eyes.

Step 5

Bake hot dogs in 375F oven for 13-17 minutes, till golden brown in color.

Step 6

Allow to cool and dip a toothpick in mustard to make their eyes. Serve.

Witch Hat Cookies

Makes

32 +/- Servings

INGREDIENTS:

☐ 2 x 1lb. pkgs. of cookies, fudge stripe ☐ 1/4 cup of strained honey, pure

☐ 1 x 9oz. bag of candy kisses, milk chocolate 1 x 4 1/2-oz. tube of decorating gel, any color except white or black

DIRECTIONS:

Step 1

Place one cookie with stripes facing down on work surface. Smear 1/8 tsp. honey on bottom of candy kiss. Secure to middle of cookie, over hole.

Step 2

Using decorating gel, pipe small bow on cookie at base of candy kiss.

Repeat with remainder of the ingredients. Serve.

Crispy Devil Brains

Preparation time: 30 minutes
Yield: 4 servings

INGREDIENTS:

- 1 cup rice cereal
- ½ cup caster sugar
- ½ cup corn syrup
- 1 cup marshmallows
- 2 tablespoons butter
- ½ cup strawberry syrup

DIRECTIONS

Step 1

In saucepan add sugar, corn syrup, marshmallows, butter and let to cook for 5-10 minutes on low heat.

Step 2

Now add in rice cereal and stir.

Step 3
Let to cool for 5 minutes.
Step 4
Now take 3-4 tablespoons of mixture in hands and shape it in the form of brain.
Step 5
Place into platter and drizzle strawberry syrup on top.
Step 6
Enjoy.

Melted Witch

Preparation time: 5 minutes
Yield: 2 servings

INGREDIENTS:
- 1 cup lychee juice
- 1 tablespoons lemon juice
- 2 tablespoons sugar syrup
- ½ cup club soda

DIRECTIONS

Step 1

In a container add all ingredients and stir.

Step 2

Add to serving glasses and serve. Enjoy.

Killing apple punch

Preparation time: 10 minutes
Yield: 2 servings

INGREDIENTS:
- [ ] 2 cups apple juice
- [ ] 1 cup red orange juice
- [ ] 2 tablespoons brown sugar
- [ ] 1 apple, sliced

DIRECTIONS

Step 1

In blender add apple juice, orange juice, brown sugar and blend well. Transfer to serving glasses and add apple slices.

Step 3

Enjoy.

Halloween Pumpkin Spice Bars

INGREDIENTS:

- 4 eggs, large
- 1 2/3 cup of granulated sugar
- 1 cup of vegetable oil
- 1 x 15-oz. can of pumpkin
- 2 cups of flour, all-purpose
- 1 tsp. of baking soda
- 2 tsp. of baking powder
- 2 tsp. of ground cinnamon
- 1 tsp. of table salt
- 1 x 3-oz. pkg. of cream cheese, light
- 1/2 cup of salted butter
- 1 tsp. of vanilla extract, pure
- 2 cups of powdered sugar

DIRECTIONS:

Step 1

Preheat the oven to 350F.

Step 2

To prepare frosting, cream the butter and cream cheese together. Add vanilla and stir. Add powdered sugar a bit at a time while beating till you have a smooth mixture.

Step 3

In medium mixing bowl, combine oil, sugar, pumpkin and eggs with electric mixer till fluffy and light.

Step 4

Sift together flour, baking soda, baking powder, salt and cinnamon. Stir into pumpkin mixture till combined well.

Step 5

Evenly spread batter in 15" x 10" jelly roll pan. Bake in 350F oven for 20-30 minutes. Remove from oven. Allow to cool, then frost, evenly spreading atop cooled bars. Slice in squares. Serve.

Mummy Hot Dogs

INGREDIENTS:

☐ 12 hot dogs, regular length (not foot-longs)
☐ 1 pkg. of crescent rolls, eight
☐ Mustard, yellow

DIRECTIONS:

Step 1

Preheat the oven to 375F. Line cookie sheet with baking paper.

Step 2

Dry the hot dogs with paper towels if they're wet.

Step 3

Using pizza or pastry cutter, cut crescent roll triangles into very thin strips.

Step 4

Pull, then stretch strips and wrap them around the hot dogs. Tuck loose dough as needed, under the bottom or back of hot dogs. Leave small openings for the eyes.

Step 5
Bake hot dogs in 375F oven for 13-17 minutes, till golden brown in color.

Step 6
Allow to cool and dip a toothpick in mustard to make their eyes. Serve.

Poison Apple Candy

Preparation time: 10 minutes
Yield: 4 servings

INGREDIENTS:

- 4 apples, cleaned
- 4 wooden sticks
- 1 cup corn syrup
- 1 cup sugar
- ¼ cup water
- 2 tablespoons maple syrup
- 1 tablespoon honey
- 2 tablespoons black jell paste food coloring

DIRECTIONS

Step 1

Insert wooden sticks into each apple and place into platter. **Step 2**

In a saucepan add sugar with water and stir till the sugar is dissolved. **Step 3** Now add corn syrup and stir continually for 1 minute. **Step 4** Turn off heat and add food colour, mix well. Let to cool a little. **Step 5** Dip apples in this mixture and place into serving platter. **Step 6** Enjoy.

Spiced Roasted Pumpkin Seeds

Preparation time: 40 minutes
Yield: 6 servings

INGREDIENTS:
- [ ] 2 cups pumpkin seeds
- [ ] ½ teaspoon slat
- [ ] ¼ teaspoon chili powder
- [ ] ¼ cup butter, melted

DIRECTIONS

Step 1
Preheat oven at 355 degrees.

Step 2
In a bowl add pumpkin seeds, chili powder, salt and melted butter, mix well to combine. **Step 3**

Transfer to baking tray and spread equally.
Step 4
Bake for 40 minutes.
Step 5
Enjoy.

Oreo Dirt Cups

Preparation time: 20 minutes
Yield: 3 servings

INGREDIENTS:

- 4 packages Oreo biscuits, crumbled
- ½ cup whipped cream
- 2 tablespoons maple syrup
- 2 tablespoons brown sugar
- 1 cup dark chocolate, chopped
- 3 gummy warms

DIRECTIONS

Step 1
In blender add chocolate, maple syrup,

brown sugar, cream and blend well. **Step 2** Ladle into serving cups and top with crushed Oreo biscuits. **Step 3** Insert gummy warms and place into fridge for 10 minutes. **Step 4** Serve and enjoy.

Glass Jelly Worms

Preparation time: 20 minutes
Yield: 4 servings

INGREDIENTS:
- 2 packages of orange jelly
- 10 gummy warms
- 2 cups water
- 5 candy creatures

DIRECTIONS

Step 1
Make the jelly with required amount of water as mentioned on its package.

Step 2
Pour mixture into serving dishes, insert gummy warms and candies as much you like.

Step 3

Place into fridge for 20-25 minutes.
Step **4**
Serve and enjoy.

Frozen Banana Ghosts

Preparation time: 10 minutes
Yield: 6 servings

INGREDIENTS:
- ☐ 3 frozen bananas, halved
- ☐ ¼ cup lemon juice
- ☐ 1 tablespoons caster sugar
- ☐ 1 tablespoon chocolate chips

DIRECTIONS

Step 1
In a bowl add lemon juice with caster sugar and dip each frozen banana in it.

Step 2
Place chocolate chips at the place of eyes and nose and lightly press them.

Step 3
Place into serving platter.

Step 4
Serve and enjoy.

Spider Sandwich Cookies

Preparation time:

10 minutes
Yield: 5 servings

INGREDIENTS:
- [ ] 8-10 chocolate cookies
- [ ] ¼ teaspoon red food color
- [ ] 1 cup cream, whipped
- [ ] ½ cup caster sugar
- [ ] 20-25 licorice, (1 inch pieces)
- [ ] Few candies for eyes

DIRECTIONS
Step 1
In a bowl add cream, sugar and food

colour, mix well.
Step 2

Spread 2 tablespoons of this mixture on cookie and top with another cookie like sandwich, repeat same steps for all cookies.

Step 3

Insert 8 liquorice strips into each cookie and top with candy eyes.
Step 4
Serve.

Mysterious Strawberries

Preparation time: 30 minutes
Yield: 7 servings

INGREDIENTS:
- [ ] 78 strawberries
- [ ] 1 cup white chocolate, melted
- [ ] ½ cup dark chocolate
- [ ] ¼ cup milk
- [ ] 1 teaspoon butter

DIRECTIONS

Step 1

Dip strawberries in white chocolate and place into freezer for 15-20 minutes.

Step 2

In a saucepan add dark chocolate with milk and butter, let to melt it well. **Step 3** Leave to cool it slightly and then transfer to piping bag.

Step 4

Now make nose and eyes with piped chocolate and place into freezer for 10 minutes again. **Step 5** Serve and enjoy.

Dead Eyeballs

Preparation time: 10 minutes
Yield: 4 servings

INGREDIENTS:
- 2 cups of vanilla ice cream
- ½ cup strawberry sauce
- 2-4 M&Ms
- Edible marker

DIRECTIONS

Step 1
Scoop out ice-cream in serving platter and top with strawberry sauce.

Step 2
Place M&Ms as eye on ice-cream and make a small dot at centre with edible marker.

Step 3
Serve immediately and enjoy.

Zombie Cocktail

Preparation time: 5 minutes
Yield: 2 servings

INGREDIENTS:

- [ ] 1 cup orange juice
- [ ] ½ cup pineapple juice
- [ ] ½ cup mango juice
- [ ] 2 tablespoons lime juice
- [ ] 1 cup crushed ice

DIRECTIONS

Step 1

In a jar add orange juice, pineapple juice, mango juice and lime juice, stir well. **Step 2**

Ladle to serving glasses and add crushed ice.

Step **3**

Place cherry or any fruit on top to decor.

Step **4**

Serve.

Good And Wicked Brew

Preparation time: 4 minutes
Yield: 2 servings

INGREDIENTS:
- 1 cup pineapple juice
- 1 cup kiwi juice
- ½ cup grapes juice
- 3̶4 cherries
- ½ cup soda water
- Few ice chunks

DIRECTIONS

Step 1
In a container add pineapple juice, soda water, kiwi juice, grapes juice and stir well.

Step 2
Add to serving glasses and add ice and

cherries.
Step 3
Serve chilled.

Blood Margarita

Preparation time: 10 minutes
Yield: 3 servings

INGREDIENTS:
- 2 cups watermelon, chunks, seeded
- 2 tablespoons lime juice
- 4 tablespoons sugar
- 4 tablespoons caster sugar
- ½ cup orange juice
- 3-4 lime slices
- 3-4 orange slices
- Few ice chunks

DIRECTIONS

Step 1
In blender add caster sugar, ice, watermelon, orange juice, lime juice and blend well.

Step 2

Strain juice and discard remaining.
Step 3
Now in a platter add sugar and roll out the rims of glasses in sugar.
Step 4
Pour juice in glasses.
Step 5
In toothpicks thread the lime an orange slices.
Step 6
Place them on each serving glass.
Step 7
Enjoy.

Scary Zombie Fingers

Preparation time: 30 minutes
Yield: 5 servings
INGREDIENTS:
- [ ] 3 cups dates, seeded
- [ ] 2 tablespoons cocoa powder
- [ ] ½ cup roasted almonds
- [ ] ½ cup pine nuts
- [ ] 2 tablespoons maple syrup
- [ ] 2 tablespoons brown sugar
- [ ] 1 cup dark chocolate, crushed
- [ ] 56 almonds sliced for garnishing

DIRECTIONS
Step 1

In blender add dates, cocoa powder, pine nuts, chocolate, almonds, brown

sugar, and maple syrup, blend well.
Step **2**
Now take 3-4 tablespoons of mixture and shape it in the form of finger, repeat same process for all fingers.

Step **3**
Place a slice of almond at the fingertip and press it lightly.
Step **4**
Transfer to freezer for 20 minutes.
Step **5**
Serve and enjoy.

Festering Apples

Preparation time:

20 minutes

Yield: 5 servings

INGREDIENTS:

- ☐ 5 apples, inside scooped out
- ☐ 1 cup white chocolate, melted
- ☐ 2 tablespoons condense milk
- ☐ 1 cup puffed rice
- ☐ 5 gummy warms
- ☐ ½ cup pineapple juice

DIRECTIONS

Step 1

In a bowl add pineapple and dip all apples in it, place into serving platter. **Step 2**

Combine condense milk, puffed rice and white chocolate.

Step 3

Now fill apples with puffed rice mixture and place 1-2 tablespoons of mixture with apples.

Step 4

Place gummy warms with apples and place into freezer for 5-10 minutes.

Step 5

Serve and enjoy.

Caramel Nut Tart

INGREDIENTS

For Bones:
- ☐ Bones mold
- ☐ 3/4 cup white chocolate candy melt

For Pastry:
- ☐ 2 cups all-purpose flour, spooned leveled, plus additional for the work surface
- ☐ ½ cup cold unsalted butter, nicely cut into tiny pieces 3 tablespoons sugar
- ☐ ¼ cup unsweetened cocoa powder 1 package cold cream cheese (8-oz), cut into small pieces ½ teaspoon kosher salt

For Filling:
- ☐ 1 teaspoon pure vanilla extract
- ☐ ½ cup heavy cream
- ☐ 2 ¼ cups nuts pretzels, chopped
- ☐ 1 ½ cups sugar
- ☐ ½ teaspoon kosher salt

For Garnish:
- ☐ Metallic dragées melted chocolate

DIRECTIONS

For Bones:

Step 1

Heat the candy melts until melted per the directions mentioned on the package. Transfer to a large, zip-top bag snip a very small hole in one of the corners. Fill the bone skeleton mold with this prepared mixture let chill for half an hour then, tap the bones out.

For Pastry:

Step 1

Pulse flour with sugar, cocoa powder salt in a food processor for a couple of times, preferably 2 to **3**

Add in the butter cubes continue to pulse for a couple of more times, until butter is like the size of peas. Add in the cream cheese continue to pulse the ingredients for 7 to 10 more times, until dough forms (feel free to add some water, as required). Using a plastic wrap; cover approximately 2/3 of the formed dough; flatten and repeat this step with the leftover dough. Let chill for a couple of hours.

Step 2

Preheat your oven to 375 F in advance. Roll a large piece of the dough on a work surface (dusted lightly with the flour) to approximately 1/8" thickness.

Fit the dough into the bottom up the sides of a tart pan, preferab ly 8x11" with removable bottom; just trim any excess. Arrange it on a large, rimmed baking sheet and line it with the parchment paper; leaving approximately 2" overhang; fill with rice or dried beans. Bake for 17 to 20 minutes approximately, until the edges are just set. Carefully lift the parchment to remove the rice or beans. Then, bake for 6 to 8 more minutes, until thebottom is dry; let cool.

Step 3

Line a large-sized rimmed baking sheet with the parchment paper. Then, roll a small piece of dough on awork surface (lightly dusted with the flour) into 1/8" thickness. Cut into various widths strips. Create a wood grain pattern by running a fork on top of the strips; transfer to your baking sheet bake for 7 to 10 minutes, until cooked through. Let cool on a wire rack on the baking sheet.

For **Filling:**
Step 1

Over medium-high heat in a medium-sized saucepan; bring sugar ½ cup of water to a boil. Decrease the heat and continue to cook for a couple of minutes, until the sugar has completely dissolved, stirring frequently.

Step 2

Remove from the heat carefully add the vanilla, cream salt in a slow stream; stir the ingredients until completely smooth. Add pretzels and nuts; stir the ingredients for a minute or two, until the caramel starts to cool down thicken slightly. Pour into the baked crust evenly spread using an offset spatula. Refrigerate for a few hours, until cold.

Step 3

Remove the base tart ring; place the tart on a large, serving platter. Garnish with chocolate bones and skeletons pastry "boards," crossing the pastry strips and ensure that it looks like boards. Add the dragées to the ends of boards (adhering them with some melted chocolate). Serve chilled and enjoy.

Guacamoldy Eyeballs

INGREDIENTS

- 2 tablespoons taco sauce, smooth, without chunks ¼ cup sour cream, low-fat
- 2 tablespoons lemon juice, fresh
- 10 eggs, large
- 4 pimiento-stuffed olives, medium
- 2 teaspoons chili powder
- 1 ½ small avocado or 1 large
- Pepper kosher salt to taste

DIRECTIONS

Step 1

First, fill your large saucepan with cold water (enough to cover the eggs); add the eggs, then bring it to a boil, over moderate heat. Once done; remove it from the heat; immediately cover the saucepan let stand for several minutes.

Step 2

In the meantime, whisk sour cream with taco sauce chili powder in a small-sized mixing bowl. Place in a large pastry bag attached with a fine tip.

Step 3

Mash the avocado with lemon juice ¼ teaspoon each of pepper salt in a separate small-sized mixing bowl. Transfer tothe resealable plastic bag; immediately cut the tip off and create a ½" opening.

Step 4

Next, drain the eggs; add them to the saucepan again; shaking the saucepan gently until all sides of the eggs is cracked. Run them under cold running tap water let cool. Once done; peel the boiled eggs and cut them lengthwise into half. Remove reserve the yolks for separate use.

Step 5

Pipe thin squiggly lines on every egg white half using the prepared sour cream mixture and ensure that they look like bloodshot eyes and pipe the prepared avocado mixture into the white; place an olive slice on top. Serve and enjoy.

Ghost Toast

Makes 12 Servings

INGREDIENTS:

- 1 pkg. of pita bread
- Optional: salt, kosher
- Optional: your choice of spices and herbs, dried or fresh

DIRECTIONS:

Step 1

Preheat the oven to 375F.

Step 2

Split the pita bread into halves through the pocket. Cut them into the proper shape with a threeinch ghost shape cookie cutter. Each pita half should make three ghosts.

Step 3

Arrange the ghosts on one or two cookie sheets. Coat them with non-stick cooking spray. Sprinkle them as desired with herbs, spices and kosher salt.

Step 4

Bake for five to eight minutes, till crisp and browned lightly. Allow to cool a bit on a wire rack. Serve.

Halloween Creepy Skull Cupcakes

Makes 24 Servings
COOKING + PREP TIME: 50 MINUTES + COOLING TIME
INGREDIENTS:
☐ 1 pkg. of devil's food cake mix
☐ 1 cup of water, filtered ☐ 3 eggs, large ☐ 1/3 cup of oil, soybean or olive

☐ 1 1/2 x 16oz. pkgs. of ready to eat, creamy chocolate frosting 1 x 7-oz. pouch of ready to eat chocolate frosting

DIRECTIONS:
Step 1
Preheat the oven to 350F. Line 2 x 12-cup

tins with muffin liners.

Step 2

Combine the water, oil, eggs, and cake mix in a large mixing bowl. Beat on the low speed with electric mixer till moistened, 25-30 seconds.

Step 3

Beat on med. speed till batter is creamy and smooth, two minutes or so. Spoon the batter in lined muffin cups, each one at 3/4 full.

Step 4

Bake in 350F oven till toothpick pushed into center comes back clean, 18-20 minutes. Remove from the oven. Cool the tins on wire rack for 12-15 minutes. Then remove the cupcakes from tins. Finish cooling on wire rack, then decorate.

Step 5

Frost cupcakes with thin layers of vanilla frosting. Refrigerate for 1/2 hour so

remainder of decorating will be easier.
Step 6

Remove the cupcakes from the refrigerator. Apply the second white frosting layer. Fill a piping bag with a round, small tip with ready to spread chocolate frosting. Draw skull faces on cupcakes. Make large-sized ovals for eyes, dots for nostrils and stitched looking smiles. Serve.

Witch Hat Cookies

INGREDIENTS:

☐ 2 x 1lb. pkgs. of cookies, fudge stripe

☐ 1/4 cup of strained honey, pure

☐ 1 x 9oz. bag of candy kisses, milk chocolate 1 x 4 1/2-oz. tube of decorating gel, any color except white or black

DIRECTIONS:
Step 1

Place one cookie with stripes facing down on work surface. Smear 1/8 tsp. honey on bottom of candy kiss. Secure to middle of cookie, over hole.

Step 2

Using decorating gel, pipe small bow on cookie at base of candy kiss. Repeat with remainder of the ingredients. Serve.

Grave Yard Taco Dip

INGREDIENTS:
- 1st layer
- 1 can of beans, refried
- 2nd layer
- 1 package of seasoning, taco
- 2 cups of sour cream, light
- 3rd layer
- 1 minced garlic clove
- 2 mashed avocados
- 2 tbsp. of mayonnaise, reduced fat
- 4th layer
- A cup of salsa– mild, medium or hot, as desired
- 5th layer (garnish)
- A bunch of chopped green onions

DIRECTIONS:
Step 1

In small-sized bowl, mix the sour cream with taco seasoning. In separate bowl, mix mayo, mashed avocados and minced garlic.

Step 2

In small-sized Pyrex® type dish, layer beans, then sour cream mixture.

Follow with avocado mixture, then salsa. Sprinkle top with chopped green onions. Chill for an hour or longer, till you are prepared to serve.

Step 3

To make tree and grave markers, cut desired shapes from two large-sized tortillas. Place cut-outs on cookie sheet lined with baking paper. Bake in 350F oven till tortillas are just browned. Text can be added with food-safe black marker. Push tree and grave markers into dip right before you serve it.

Pumpkin Cinnamon Halloween Cookies

INGREDIENTS:
- 2 cups of shortening
- 2 cups of canned pumpkin
- 2 eggs, whole, large
- 1 1/2 tsp. of ground cinnamon
- 1 tsp. of table salt
- 4 cups of flour, all-purpose
- 1 cup of granulated sugar
- 6 tbsp. of butter, salted
- 8 tbsp. of milk, 2%
- 2 cups of powdered sugar
- 1 1/2 tsp. of vanilla extract, pure
- 1 cup of brown sugar
- 2 tsp. of baking soda or other leavening agent

DIRECTIONS:
Step 1

Cream the shortening, pumpkin and granulated sugar. Add the eggs and combine thoroughly. Sift flour, salt, cinnamon and baking soda together. Add this to the pumpkin sugar mixture. Combine well.

Step 2

Use a spoon to drop cookies on cookie sheet. Bake in 350F oven for 10 minutes.

Step 3

To prepare the frosting, cook the milk, brown sugar and butter till dissolved. Allow to cool. Add vanilla and powdered sugar. Spread on cookies and serve.

www.ingramcontent.com/pod-product-compliance
Lightning Source LLC
Chambersburg PA
CBHW050403120526
44590CB00015B/1813